Concert and Contest COLLECTION

Compiled and Edited by **H. VOXMAN**

for

Eb or BBb BASS (Tuba-Sousaphone) **with piano accompaniment**

CONTENTS

RUBANK®

HAL•LEONARD® CORPORATION
7777 W BLUEMOUND RD PO BOX 13819 MILWAUKEE, WI 53213

T0071539

Sarabanda and Gavotta

Eb or BBb Bass

A. CORELLI
Transcribed by H. Voxman

Waltz and Galop
from Petite Suite

Eb or BBb Bass

D. KABALEVSKY
Transcribed by H. Voxman

Two Short Pieces

E♭ or BB♭ Bass

G. F. HANDEL
Transcribed by H. Voxman

ARIA (Rinaldo)

Premier Solo de Concours

Eb or BBb Bass

RENÉ MANIET
Transcribed by H. Voxman

Largo and Allegro

E♭ or BB♭ Bass

Continuo realized
by R. Hervig

B. MARCELLO
Transcribed by H. Voxman

Air Gai

E♭ or BB♭ Bass

G. P. BERLIOZ
Transcribed by H. Voxman

Andante and Allegro

Eb or BBb Bass

ROBERT CLÉRISSE
Transcribed by H. Voxman

Andante Cantabile
from Concerto

Eb or BBb Bass

N. RIMSKY - KORSAKOV
Transcribed by H. Voxman

Persiflage

Eb or BBb Bass

PAUL KOEPKE

Adagio and Allegro
from Sonata No. 7

Eb or BBb Bass

Continuo realized
by R. Hervig

G. F. HANDEL
Transcribed by H. Voxman

First Movement
from Concerto for Horn

Eb or BBb Bass

W. A. MOZART
Transcribed by H. Voxman

Serenade and Scherzo

Eb or BBb Bass

LEROY OSTRANSKY

Morceau de Concours

Eb Bass

G. ALARY, Op. 57
Transcribed by H. Voxman

Adagio and Finale
from Concertino

BB♭ Bass

CHARLES GAUCET
Transcribed by H. Voxman

FINALE